Traveling Empty

Traveling Empty

for Becca —

You've been such a help along the way,
& you make SMOL SING — & & DRME TOO ,
I'm grateful for your PERE +
Loving ness — and just plain
grateful to you!
Thinking peace and Pxxxe .

Poems by Susan Dewitt, CSJP

Love,

Susam —

2019

Kenmare Press
Englewood Cliffs, New Jersey

Library of Congress Control Number: 2019911539

ISBN: 978-0-359-80639-3

eISBN: 978-0-359-81094-9

Kenmare Press
An imprint of the Sisters of St. Joseph of Peace
399 Hudson Terrace
Englewood Cliffs, New Jersey 07632

www.csjp.org

For the Sisters of St. Joseph of Peace

We commit ourselves to promote peace
in family life, in the church, and in society.
We strive to respect the dignity of all persons,
to value the gifts of creation,
and to confront oppressive situations.
We respond to God's people in need
and promote social justice
as a way to peace.

Constitutions of the Sisters of St. Joseph of Peace, 11

ACKNOWLEDGEMENTS

And now in age I bud again,
After so many deaths I live and write;
*   I once more smell the dew and rain,*
And relish versing. Oh, my only light,
*   It cannot be*
*   That I am [s]he*
*   On whom thy tempests fell all night.*

                  George Herbert, "The Flower"

Thank you first and last of all to the Sisters of St. Joseph of Peace who have given me cause and time and space to write over these last 27 years, and now are publishing this book of poems. Soon after I entered the community, I knew the truth of George Herbert's words: after a long fallow spell, my joy in words and poems came alive again, and here is the result. Almost all of these poems were written during my years as a sister, and with the loving support of my community.

Many of these poems were written for meetings of my writers' group, Elsie's Salon, and shared with my dear friends and collaborators Janet Hasselblad, Cherry Johnson, Linda Mack, Ruth Pettis, and occasionally Jaila Hansen. Some of the most recent were written during Hugo House's Poetry II workshop, led by Keetje Kuipers.

A 30-day retreat with Father Andy Dufner, S.J. at the Nestucca Sanctuary gave birth to many poems including "Annunciation," my attempt at Ignatian role-playing. Others come from my years at Jubilee Women's Center, where women facing crisis and homelessness have found housing and support since 1984. A few reflect my four years in El Salvador with PazSalud, the El Salvador Health Mission of PeaceHealth and the Sisters of St. Joseph of Peace. And some are daily prayer.

"Traveling Empty" was published in the *Cistercian Studies Quarterly*; "Petitions to St. Therese" was published in *Pontoon*; and a number of these poems have been published in *PeaceTimes and Living Peace*, journals of the Sisters of St. Joseph of Peace.

Deep thanks to my lifelong friend, Roger Whitlock, for permission to use his watercolor of *Useless Bay, Whidbey 1* for the cover. Roger reminds me that at Whitman College he designed the cover for our literary magazine, to which I contributed many poems, so this is a beautiful continuance.

And finally thanks to the giver of all gifts:

A Meditation on Psalm 92

How great your works, O holy One,
how deep your purpose.
I need to know that somewhere
the wicked get punished:
they seem to do well here and now.
You have a problem with my eyes,
my judgement?
The wicked root in me and punish.
The just root in me and flourish.
It's hard, some days, to tell the difference.
It's hard, some days, to bear fruit
though I dwell in your courts, O Beloved,
though I am planted in your house.

CONTENTS

CONTENTS *[Continued]*

Traveling Empty

Breath by Breath

Sweet spirit breather come and use
these rotten lungs. A few more years
of in and out, a few more million
breaths. May I breathe in morning coffee and the scent
rising from the lemons that fell into the patio
last night, the smoke from Dinora's next-door cooking,
smell of wet earth, bean soup, the flat hot steam
of new tortillas, wine and hot chocolate, pupusas,
sun trapped in the cotton of my sheets.

I breathe in.

Spirit use me, breath by every breath,
to talk through everyday, the joy and rub
of fellowship. *Ayúdame, que mi lengua sea
capaz de la arquitectura y la música del español,*
may I speak this language of the courts and angels
with respect, with love. Open my voice,
that poor, hoarse thing, that rough rumble,
crow call, *hazme un instrumento de tu paz*
may my words become a channel of your peace.

I breathe out.

Spirit, use me up. Since I woke up at night at five
years old, no breath to speak of, the good air
whistling through narrowed passageways, I've known
how great that gift, that movement in and out, exchange:
taking in the breath of strangers, saints and villains,
breath of the lemon tree, wood smoke;
giving back a breath shaped and smelling of me,
a word my lips have shaped, or yours.
Let me breathe until it is time and then be done
willingly.

I breathe.

The Low Road Blues
(for Pat D'Andrea)

If I could go,
if I had a car and could take off,
I'd drive all the back roads to New Mexico,
check out the chili in the tired cafes
in all the dirt road towns in southern Idaho,
drink gin in Utah,
sing at the top of my off-pitch voice
Amazing Grace
in some patched motel in Moab,
Monticello, or Mexican Hat,
rattle through the four corners
on a wobbling wheel and a stuck clutch,
get fry bread in Shiprock,
cigarettes and a six pack in a joint at the edge of
        the res,
head on down to Cuba on bald tires
in a cloud of burning oil,
limp in to Bernalillo
with a hole in the radiator and a rat's nest
in the back seat,
and lurch up to Santa Fe,
held together by duct tape, hope
and the insects stuck to the windshield,
from nowhere, going nowhere.

And you would take me in.

Trees of the Forest Shout for Joy

Fierce as a lover, wind works the tree,
pulls out dead branches, needles, moss.

Wind plays the tree harp, murmurs,
creak of wood on wood, full howls.

Wind beats on the tree
the breath of other places
where the tree has only one.

Wind takes the tree
on, sending her children
into the far.

Tree gives the wind a voice.

What joy, what faithful partnership:
a psalm breathed,
a psalm rooted.

Monkey Mind

Goes everywhere, can't keep still a minute,
goes after a thought, pursuing it, hunting it down,
leaping over fences and into strange fields after it,
tying it with strings and ribbons and only then
noticing the water boiling over on the stove,
the piles of books around the room –
that book! let's check it out, and
what'm I making for dinner? I forgot to write that check
but I wonder what's going on with Annie,
I never hear from her, and there's a paper on the floor,
better see what it says, oh a pottery sale, maybe I'll just
eat and go to sleep, but what's going on in Mexico?
Is the rice burned? I remember reading about
a good exercise program and STOP

PING
to sit to be breathing
the flame trembles over the candle
light makes a home in the orchard
outside my window in
side my body
light
NING AND GO

wonder if I'll see the raccoon today?
Do I still have an egg in the kitchen?
I need to clean up,
my friends are coming over tonight and
there's an article in the paper about Social Security,
the crossword to finish, the news to listen to,
the garbage to take OUT

SIDE on the quiet side of forever
the sunset waits. Stop and I'll go.

Traveling Empty

A long way north from Santa Fe
a dirt road branches into nowhere,
no signpost helping you. Take the road,
even if you don't know where it's going but away
from work lists, meetings and the ordinary
civilities we die in. Take the road
a long way up the Rio Chama canyon
between sagebrush and rabbitbrush,
between pink and saffron cliffs,
through arroyos, dust, deep ruts,
a road leading out of what you think you know
until you're lost enough to come
to Christ in the Desert in the high plains
quiet air.

Leave the car at the gate with the rest
of the troubles buzzing in your head
and walk a long path to the chapel,
an earth cave full of light. John Baptist
guards your quiet and the Virgin waits
to hear the Word forever. Pure light
unfolds the cliffs. A red-tailed hawk circles
the high windows. A monk puts chamisa
in an earthenware bowl. Scripture is open
to the word you need to hear.

Then you need to find the way
back home, to your ordinary muddled house
like the one I live in, commodious,
unbeautiful, on an ordinary, middle-class street
in a city planned for comforts, not for prayer, full
of voices, oil slicks, sirens, shops, fears.
Travel back empty, bring back
only what you cannot hold: the light,
the track of the red-tailed hawk,
silence unfolding the word.

Gema's Garden

Gema's Garden

Once there was a garden in the middle of my house
in Suchitoto, El Salvador,
and in it the lemon tree I always longed for,
lemon flowers tasting of the fruit to come,
buckets of lemons in full season,
shade from the sun, protection from the rain,
healthy without my help. The nance flourished too,
red berries, too sweet for me,
beloved by my Salvadoran friends,
and the peace plant, the impatiens,
the two big ficus in enormous pots,
bougainvillea and hibiscus in the sunniest corner.
Butterflies came with the rains,
and I thought of you, Gema,
wise child, princesa, carrying your lupus
seed of death.
I never knew how to be a gardener
in my most beautiful garden
in the middle of my house
in Suchitoto, El Salvador.
Small worms curled the leaves of the ficus
and I never could wash them away.
The orchids never flowered again
after my friends brought them to me
and put them in the right place on the nance's trunk,
and the vegetables I tried to raise from seed –
tomatoes, kale, amaranth – came up and died.
I'd get up at three in the morning, Gema,
to get you to the doctors in San Salvador,
to get you medicines that helped and then
that poisoned you. I wanted to take you home,
my other home,
where someone would give you gringo medicine
to magic you well.
I never could.
I wanted to change your life
when I couldn't even keep the bougainvillea

and hibiscus safe from the leaf cutters
who one day ate every leaf and left the branches bare.
They knew how to grow new leaves.
You could not,
and I drove to pick up your mother
and your small body in a bag
and drove for two hours
to take you to the funeraria,
where they found you a small, white casket,
and we made a procession, very slow,
to lay you in the ground.
Your mother and your sisters and your brother gathered
    round
and your grandparents and all the aunts and uncles and
    cousins
and their friends. I was there, too.
Later we put a fence around your grave
and planted roses, Gema, princesa,
to be your garden.
That night bats flew
through the garden in the middle of my house
in Suchitoto, El Salvador,
and an iguana
climbed into the lemon tree. Princesa,
your people know how to make a garden,
how to welcome the butterflies, the bats,
how to share life with the ants and scorpions,
what could be done and what could not,
how to let go
of all they hold most dear.
I never knew.
Princesa, Gema, the roses grow around your grave,
you live in my memory
like the lemon tree
still growing in the garden in the middle of the house
that once was mine.

Spring Harvest

Cold wet gray March. I'm digging
in a garden not my own,
getting the beds ready for seed,
for the hope of hot summer.
I turn up dirt, the roots of weeds and grasses,
an old glass bottle, tags from last year's garden,
great lumps of soft dark soil, two worms,
and something red. . . a new potato
firm, round, perfect, ready for harvest,
unlikely as an Easter egg,
but there's another and another,
not one in every spadeful, but
every once in a while, as fresh and edible
as daily bread, as grace,
harvested
where I did not plant.

The Kindom of Heaven

is like
the shade under the cedar tree
where a rabbit browses
on new fern shoots and buttercups
safely out of the eyeshot
of eagles

is like
friends meeting again
after long absence, smiling
and awkward, asking
"How are you?"
"How are you?" "How..."

is like
that moment in the movies
when a couple pulls away
from the crowded dance floor,
from the noise and sweat of the crowd
opens a door and waltzes
into silence, darkness,
the pulse of stars.

is like
rain falling into a lake,
each waterdrop making a circle,
each circle overlapping other circles
all circles diminishing into the fullness
of water.

Weeds

put roots down under the sidewalk,
under a canopy of proper plants, in overgrown corners,
in disorder.
These send out leaves like spies
on long green cords,
send down roots to last,
send up pure yellow flowers,
these demon   buttercups
these innocent, childgame plants
these enemies.
I see them in my sleep, these buttercups,

intruders that I must root out,
and I who say how much,
how much I love
the life in everything
go after buttercups
with a long sharp prod
to pull the roots out too.

The garden's to be a proper place,
plants under control growing
where I set them, heather,
rhododendron, St. John's wort,
thyme, and I'm let pretend
that I'm the tyrant here,
shouting   off
    with their heads   out
    with their roots
to these lowlife interlopers,
these unwashed weeds that crop up everywhere,
these homeless begging for a place to grow.

I'm the tyrant here: go home
to all the places where a weed belongs,
to cracks in sidewalks, vacant lots, edges
of a compost heap, a stream, a bit of meadow,
somewhere else,
(make glad the day with yellow flowers)
not here.

The Call

In Christ all things hold together. Col 1:17

Alder and fir lean into the wind,
streaked, whorled in the embrace of air.
Sparrows are courting. It's wet, but
it's spring. The firstborn of all creation
holds the pattern that we dance in,
tree shaping air, sparrow
singing the branches, all creation
bowing and swaying
as I do now.

The gardener knows
and the clerk at the store,
the old man at the post office
knows the pattern, how we bow and sway
to touch each other, touch the earth,
touch our wholeness,
hidden with the sparrow's eggs
in the mind of Christ.

Let me also dance
in you, beloved,
let me take my part
in the pattern
of which you are the whole.

The Gardener's Prayer

Beloved, bless
this day, the clouds
piling up over us, weeds
thriving in the gardens,
bless my hope
to create a clean and perfect garden
and my failure.
You who bless chaos
from which all order rises,
embrace the slug,
chickweed, crabgrass, aphids,
me.

Weathering

From out of the fog's
enormous space
a fencepost clears and then
an edge of the road, grasses,
a treetrunk lifts, slowly
green returns,
the taste of oranges,
speed, tomorrow.

Getting through fog asks patience,
asks belief
that underneath the soft blanket,
the echoing wet grayness,
lies a familiar world of heft and color,
the taste of oranges.

Weathering fog
I choose to doubt
its permanence
who once spent years
lost in enormous grayspace.
I look for the edge of the road
coming clean
into the light.

Unmanageable

No containing
the fountain of green leaves
pouring from the dry
moss-covered, brittle
elderberry,
no counting
the thin new leaves
of lupine, wild cucumber,
foxtail,
we cannot manage

                spring,
we proud creatures,
who like to manage forests,
rivers, plains.
Resurrection happens
when we're not looking:
the tomb springs open

               empty and life
calls to us from somewhere else
where the salmonberry blooms
and the ruby throated hummingbird
drinks from its
(innumerable)
magenta flowers.

Pearly Everlasting
(for Judith Stoloff)

Nothing I have to do or
to undo
matters this Monday morning
while Pearly Everlasting
blooms on the slopes of Mother Mountain.

                              Names
Trefoil Foamflower
Little Pipsissewa
Large Mountain Monkey Flower
have their own attraction   recall a picture
(bottom left) of some thing

                    the float of small white petals
                    nameless.

Bluebells, blueberries, huckleberries,
salmonberries, elderberries, fireweed,
fitweed   beautiful upon the mountains,
the feet of one
                    bringing good news,
nameless
as seed in wet ground.

Fish Biting

Lake Texoma, Oklahoma.

A secret the old man told me:
the fish are biting on cheese,
Velveeta cheese,
and that's all they'll take today,
Velveeta cheese
on the end of a line
held by a patient old man
with a six pack and cigarettes
and three friends in a flatbottomed barge
and nothing better,
nothing better to do,
nothing better to do all day
than wait in the sun for the catfish to rise
to the bite of Velveeta cheese.

The Languages of Women

Homecoming, for Liz

While we pulled your things out of a truck
that held enough furniture for a three
bedroom home all to be fit somehow
in this one bedroom and small apartment

while we struggled with the old dolly
and a cart brought out from somewhere
in these Housing Authority apartments
and with all your boxes upon boxes

that you packed so carefully away paying for
the storage month after month when you didn't
have enough for food or to get your hair done
and had to use the straightening iron

and I made you do it in the basement (because
of fire danger) until you told me how it was unfair
that white women kept their hair dryers upstairs
and you had to do your hair (that most private

rite) in public in the basement like a servant,
like a slave and you were right because I never
thought about the intricate histories of
black hair you were right

to claim your dignity and the pride
of your family what your mother told you
about how to keep yourself when you had no
money at all and I apologized who never meant,

who never meant any evil but did it anyway –
while we were taking in the dressers
the two huge sofas the TV the dining
table while our backs were cracking from the loads

set free from storage, they sat out front
your new neighbors the old black man
two old black women and watched
as though they could never see enough

while two white women carried in your goods.

Lost Girls

The lost girls come to visit
at two in the morning
carrying the small claims of their lives,
the ones who were never loved
or never loved enough,
so many.

Dorothy died neglected,
Margaret took her own life,
Betty stopped taking pills,
Kate started drinking,
Jan got in fights,
Ellie sold dope
out of her bedroom window
in the old convent,
so many
who are not success stories
I can put on white bond paper
for the donors and foundations.

Lou disappeared,
Joan went back to the streets,
May went back to the man
who knocked her across the room,
broke her head open so she can't
read anymore, do math, do anything,
May thinks she's too dumb now
for anyone else.
I love her
but I can't keep her
from harm.
At two in the morning
she comes to visit
and I ask her
how I could have helped.

Lily comes who talked to herself in many voices,
Mindy, who gave me a sign when she left
that said "Dangerous: Explosives,"
and Miriam, who danced through the house
black woman singing joy,
free woman, who could preach
the best sermons I ever heard
about the courage to change,
the wisdom to know the difference,
Miriam, who loved all of us,
loved her grandbabies, loved being clean,
played dominoes at the top of her voice,
who went to the ocean for the first time
at forty-seven,
is doing drugs again,
begging for money, food,
sleeping out on the streets.

My lost darling,
my friend,
at two o'clock in the morning
I hear your laugh.
You once were found,
but now you're lost.
Come back.
Come back.
Come home.

The Good Girl

So good she was, so sweet, always
smiling gently   never
shouting or cussing or cracking dirty jokes
with the bad girls on the porch
enough to make your teeth ache, her goodness,
a single note held thinly and without
resonance.
                    Only at night, through the nightmares,
the bad girl rose up in her like a demon, took her clothes off,
yelled, fought, cursed.

                    Exorcism
didn't work, marriage
fell into the hole where she wasn't, doctors
peered into the tracings of her sleep and found the disconnect,
the mad, bad cells crouched in a corner,
raising trouble, raising hell

                              and took them out.

Now she is good all through and thin as glass,
only she can't remember names, the names of friends
or streets or recipes, or curses
                              the tough particulars
that rope us to the world.

                    The bad girl
curled around the names. They went out with her.

Crone Round

My unused womb's used up now,
shriveled like an old pear,
a bag with nothing in it, without

seed, without center, bare
and empty flesh. And I am round
and wrinkled, an old apple. I dare

not take these images too far – around
here we know how to make use of the old,
the seed and vine, turned back into the ground

to sprout again as wheat, as bread we hold,
fermented into wine we pour and pass.
And I, though out of use, will learn that mold

is fruitful too, a turning, an embrace
of earth to earth. If I am closer now
to Brother Death, becoming earth and grass,

then let me dance, unlimberly and slow,
the crone's great dance that bends me down and low
until I kiss the earth and die and grow.

Geocentricity

In theology class, the professor insisted
on transcendence, reaching up beyond ourselves
to God we'd never catch, unless, by levitation,
God and my soul meet in some lacy cloud,
a trance of neverwhere, in sweet retirement from
this rough and dirty world. More likely that I'd miss.
Gravity ties me down to this world,
this body's daily nudgings, love and food and sleep

Who'd want to rhumba with a distant God,
omnipotent, omniscient, omnipresent, far away?
I won't go dancing on that airy bridge.
I'll gambol with a God who grounds herself
in chickadees and cabbages and apple trees,
sweet kindoms of the curved and turning earth.

The Cook Vanishes

Simone de Beauvoir disapproved of woman's work.
It must always be done again, never accomplished once and
forever, unlike an essay or a painting.

A woman cooks who at other times
has read theology and studied
disorders of the mind.

She is completely absorbed.
She chops mushrooms
with a newly sharpened knife.

No thought lurks among
the stems of green onions,
the curled mushroom caps.

No one holds the knife, no one
among the yellow peppers, the cilantro leaves,
the tight wrapped onion bulbs.

With no where to be but here
the cook vanishes
among the mushrooms.

Resistance

We are the stuck drawer, the door
that will not yield to any key. We
are a breathing wall of women, men
children, strangers who have never met,
best friends, new friends. We are the wall
that cannot be unbuilt or overcome,
We are the locked door only fools
can enter, only the lost
can find.

January, 2017

Bus Riders

I am the old woman with more bundles
than she can manage sitting next to the young man
full of his heat who tries a line on the black woman,
young, really a girl, sitting ahead of him. Nothing
comes of it. She laughs with her girlfriend.
A seat comes open and I move my bundles there,
keeping him in view
as he sniffs his underarms to find out if he's stinking,
pulls his hat over his eyes, pretends to be asleep.

                          No, I want to say,
you smell sweet as teen spirit, sweat and smoke,
the sting of desire. Don't you know that if you kiss
a lumpy old woman, take her in your arms with all
her bags, she'll turn into a supermodel?

                          Bless you,
nobody taught you the Wife of Bath's Tale. You'll have to wrestle
your desire, your humiliation into some other story
you can take home with you when we reach your stop
to drown the imagined noise of women laughing.
Bluebeard, perhaps? Ted Bundy?

                          Don't take it that way.
Give an old woman a kiss. You'll be surprised.

The Languages of Women

1.

I had the biopsy last week, she said.
They treated me like a car getting a lube job,
put me face down on a table with a hole cut into it
so my breast hung through and they worked on it from below.
I'd have hated that,
but there was a woman who stood by my shoulder,
massaged my back, told me what was happening,
and that made all the difference.

2.

Solomon knew he was pledged
to the Master of the Universe, the Lord of Hosts,
the Mighty One of Jacob,
but his wives remembered the goddess
in the green groves, the old hilltop places,
ceremonies of the full moon;
they remembered their mothers' stories and
(gently, peaceably, inexorably) his seven hundred wives
(many foreign; each of whom he loved)
whispered into his aging ears,
led him astray.

3.

You go Thursday, and I'll drop in on Friday,
said my sister, arranging our daily times with Mother,
who more and more forgot which day it was, and sometimes
who we were. We nattered about my brother, who should come
more often, who should share this work with us,
but, my sister said, men just don't know how to be

when someone's sick. My sons won't know what to do with me
when I'm wandering in confusion, but my daughters-in-law,
they'll know to make a cup of tea and see my clothes are clean,
brush my hair and hug me, listen to my wanderings,
tell me all is well.

4.

Yang Huanyi died in her 90s,
in Jiangyong, Hunan Province, China, the last woman
who wrote and spoke Nüshu, an enigmatic language
invented by women, used only by women.
She left behind a small chest of manuscripts, poems,

stories, cures, ceremonies of the full moon, that no one now can read.

Her great-granddaughter, rubbing her bent and aching lily feet,
listened to the babble of lost words and cried with her
and told her all is well.

Conversations with the Holy Ones

Speaking in Miracles

I threw a maraschino cherry on the compost heap
and found it three months later all unchanged,
cherry red, cherry ripe,
I haven't eaten maraschino cherries since.

Some saints are like that. They're unearthed
all clean and uncorrupted, smelling sweet as roses,
as if perfection dwelt in them
and not bacteria.

Unstained by the world.

But surely there were times when diggers
looking for holy bones would find instead
a heap of dirt or humus, nothing left
but ground to grow a tree on,

as a tree has grown from the compost heap
my mother kept for thirty years:
from the onion skins, coffee grounds, the egg shells
and grapefruit rinds –

an explosion of green.

Surely some saints have chosen
to flower in their deaths,
to hold a festival with worms and seeds,
be clay, be water, be at home in earth,

speaking in miracles of leaf and flower.

Petitions to St. Thérèse

1. Closing Down
   (for Mark)

Nothing I can do for you
or to you
anymore. The wheel and round
of our civility is cracked.
Two years I've carried the thought of you
with me, the prayer of you
has risen through me. We were friends
some ways, and some ways not. You showed me
your icon of Thérèse, told me how she sent you roses
in a dream. I told you
about entering my new life,
I brought you roses from St. Mary's garden.
Now you've done
with me what's in your power to do:
turned me out of my office,
rejected me
shaking with the anger
of a young man who's dying
and can do nothing about it.
And there's nothing I can do for you
but let you go,
let go the words I never spoke,
I'll stay with you to the end,
and give you all that's in my power to give
release, sweet freedom, love,
a prayer:
Thérèse, send down another rose.

Petitions to St. Thérèse

2. The Boy among Roses

Thérèse, Thérèse, it's time.

Float down some roses to my sick, sad friend
who needs a miracle.

Once he was young and sweet,
a boy among roses in a Kansas town,

now the life is coughing out of him.
He's burning as you did once.

No one would pray to you for long life.
I'm asking only for a rose,

rapture of petals crowding into light,
excess and gaudy splendor,

flutter of silk, the touch of skin on skin,
summer's scent, the crimson bed of joy.

May he know himself loved before the dying thickens.
Fold him into the heart of your rose.

Petitions to St. Thérèse

3. A Farewell

I bring you yellow roses
in the nursing home where you lie dying,
June roses drooping from the hot car.
You smell them one last time,
and tell me to set them over on a table
where you cannot see them, having lost
your seeing somewhere in the night.

Later, in the silence of your dying,
I pull your body toward me
for the nurse to change the sheets,
your slightness gone into dead weight,
your naked legs sprawled out,
I hold your body as a mother
holds her dead child.

Four years I've known you and this is the end.
I speak the prayers for you,
the Hail Marys that you loved to say,
I speak my love into your helpless
silence. I speak farewell to you
whose eyes will soon be opened, who will rise
and sing.

My dear, my difficult, contrary friend,
put down your fears and be at peace at last.
There's just a step, and you must take it now,
out of this last retreat, up from the pain
to where the angels wait for you,
saints rise to greet you, and Thérèse
has roses for you that will never die.

Petitions to St. Thérèse

4. For Mark, Remembering

The roses are falling, Mark,
turning brown at the edges, fading
the leaves blotched with mildew.
It is time to be done with the roses,
but I will find one or two
alive enough to take
to your unmarked place in Calvary,
to bring a rose to your ashes.

I still hear your voice, the way
you said my name.
I remember your shopping lists
with brand names all spelled out –
Stouffer's Chicken Pot Pie, Ocean Spray
Cranberry Juice, the 32 ounce size,
two thick cut pork chops,
three Braeburn apples and Post
Oat Bran Flakes.
I miss the demands you made on me
in Jesus' name, in
the name of love,
you, flaming queen, flouncing out the door,
ahead of me, the rules
for men and women did not apply
to you or me, your own rules
were far stricter. I never was good enough,
nobody was, not your mother or lovers
or friends. Everybody failed you,
sniffed into secrets (so you thought),
forgot appointments (my particular sin), or
made demands on you. You fired us all, one
after one.

In the name of love
you came back to us, imperfect
friend, to give us your death
and yourself.

Don took your Norfolk pine,
Leroy your Amaryllis,
I have two plants I can't put names to,
a crowding of green leaves.
Leroy says your Amaryllis bloomed
the day of your burial,
and in my house exotic flowers
unfolded from your pot of green leaves.

I know, I thought I knew, that dying
we let go our individual lives
and become one.
I find I can't imagine you that way,
or anyone. I miss you.
You were so particular. Thank you
for the flowers.

Midwives

(For Cherry and Marilyn Johnson)

Nothing to be done, they said, and so you did
the nothing that costs everything:
bathing, cleaning, feeding, trying to explain
why this should be happening to her, "to me?"
getting up ten times a night or more
to keep her safe in bed, trying to explain
why she couldn't walk, which she accepted
for five minutes, then forgot again,
spending everything you had and more
as she folded in on herself, body
that sheltered you nine months shrinking
toward another birth.

    Dark, it is dark now, she is walking
    by some imagined light down
    to the river, to the dock, to the small boat.
    Dark, silent, alone. She sits in the boat.
    The boat moves into the river, silent, no
    one steering. For a long time.

    And the light.
    Light after silence. The boat fades.
    She swims,
    fish among fish, in the river of her death
    reborn
    and for a moment understanding
    everything, swims
    into the light.

And you midwives, you heroes, emptied of everything,
began to clean the room of her photos and memories,
knowing she did not need them any more
now you had walked her home.

Conversations
(For Denise Levertov)

In dark December we walk in God's silence

pared to the bone and repaired,
patched like old kettles.

In dark December you are skin and bone
and hungry heart. Pain eats you. Your long
beautiful hands thin out, bone bare.

A crise de foi, you explain, a crisis
of faith and medicine has laid you down
upon your couch. The pills you have not taken,
the food you have not eaten

conspire against you. Jesus is distant
and our ugly churches cannot speak the mystery
of light. You walk in God's silence,
poet, guardian of the word,
toward the year's darkest day and death

among friends and poems
on a day of winter sunshine
when you turn inward, curl around
last words

and go to meet that distant father
now at home and ready to explain
everything. What conversation

will reveal the secrets of the great blue heron
and the intimacies of the vine leaves?

What music tunes the clouds around the mountain?

Passing the Cup
(for the community at St. Patrick's, Seattle)

Two nails chipped, palms
peeling wax from Saturday's floor, a hangnail
and a scar where I cut through bread
into a finger – my hands aren't pretty,
dry hands beginning now
to wrinkle, swell around the knuckle,
hands which have been in every crevice,
every secret place, knowing
intricate things.

In these used hands a glass cup filled with Christ
for other knowing, secret, well-used hands
to take. One man cups his hand over mine,
as gentle as a lover. These are all my lovers,
the shy man turning away as he takes the cup, the girl
in pigtails very serious, the deafblind man
with his delicate and talking hands, the tall woman
who looks at me to say Amen,
the Blood of Christ
passing from hand to hand, so carefully,
from hand
to hand, the one
who has no hands but ours.

One by one
I look at each and name
the Blood of Christ I give,
the Blood of Christ I see before me,
Christ alive this gray and beautiful morning
in all these battered and beloved hands.

Sharing the Trail

Sitting on a rock above the lake, above the green valley
I pull out lunch, pleased that I've come this far.
Above me, a step: I turn to see a mountain goat
stopping to graze along the path, perhaps ten feet from me,
massive, serene, white, male and in my way.
I remember the naturalist's story last night
about the doctor who brought in mountain goat photos
and loved them because the goat was smiling. He'd taken
lots of shots. That goat wasn't happy, she said.
That goat was scared and angry, baring his teeth. All those photos!
Probably that goat went celibate last year.

This goat who wanders in to my view isn't smiling,
seems mostly intent on the summer grasses,
but when I stand he stands sideways to me across the path
(another sign of agression, says the naturalist).
I stand sideways too, and keep my eyes down, and talk
in a mellow mumble about meaning no harm and could I
just walk up the path a bit and how I hope he'll stay,
enjoy the grass and father many children.
After a bit of this, he moves aside just far enough
for me to pass out of reach of his sharp horns and hoofs.

I walk past him and up to the spring
where I pause again and see
he's come grazing after me and is
just downhill and looking conversational. Perhaps
he likes my voice the way I like his presence or perhaps
we're just two celibates grazing together, he and I,
reaching across the barriers as creatures can do,
one to the other, sharing the trail and the tale.

Annunciation

Mary's was not the first house
the angel stopped at. No, he had been travelling
for days, walking around the Galilee,
talking to young women (or trying to talk):
one braiding her hair in a new
and most intricate fashion, too absorbed to see
the angel vibrating at the edge of her vision; one
so busy minding her small sisters and brothers
that she had no time for a word; and one weeping so hard
she couldn't hear the angel's soft voice
(that sounded like the wind in olive leaves)
saying, "Excuse me, could we talk?"
No luck at all. The angel was weary,
bedraggled, but the Holy One
had been clear: keep looking, you'll know
when you find her. And there,
in the last orchard in Nazareth,
a woman (perhaps not the youngest,
the most beautiful) has forgotten the laundry,
listening to the wind in the olive leaves
and the cry of the dove. Carefully, the angel pauses,
shakes out his wings, beats off the dust
of all of Nazareth and clears his throat
"Hail," he says softly, "Mary."

Meditation on the Face of Christ

Your face

shifts in my heart.
So many eyes
look out of yours,
so many faces –
I cannot one you,
own you.

The smell of you
fills creation
like fresh earth turned up,
like sweetgrass burning,
pinyon, honeysuckle,
cinnamon, orange,
clove.
You come to me
smelling like a lover,
like a king,

dressed in vine leaves,
crowned with basil
and sweet bay.
I cannot hold you
even for a minute,
I cannot hold you
from the shadow
(fast approaching)
of your death.

First Session

How can I find hope?

Take off your coat and sit down. Sit
down. Not on the couch. There's a straight-backed
wooden chair. Sit there. Wait until
you can breathe more easily. Let your heart
calm down a little. Now. What do you seek?

How can I find hope?

Remember the way you came here, driving
or driven, all the lights on in the winter dark:
did you see anything unexpected? A blue roof?
A snowy owl? A ragged man with a backpack?
Did a red hound chase the car? Were primroses blooming
early in a yard you passed? Have you seen
nothing?

Nothing. But what can I do? How can I find hope?

Where were you when you were seeing nothing
along the way?

I was still at work, I was chewing over my day's cud –
people, confusion, bad news, a headache, worry –
I was watching the traffic, listening to the news.
What are you getting at? What can I do?
How can I find hope?

Stay seated, please. Don't be alarmed.
Breathe slowly and again. Notice
this moment full of silences. Notice your breath
and those thoughts chasing each other around –
notice them too, as you might notice
a red hound, a snowy owl, a ragged man. Notice
the color of your shoes, the feel of the chair
on your backside, rumbles of digestion.

All very fine, all calming, but irrelevant. In the face

of war, earthquakes, poverty, outrages, stupidity, the rape
of earth, the loss of human kindness,
how can I find hope?

Try speaking softly. Hope
is a story you tell yourself as despair
is also a story you tell yourself. Try living
for a minute without stories. Breathe
and let go of them all. You will find
you hardly recognize yourself. You will find
yourself shifting, dispersing. You will breathe
unimagined air. You will find

Hope?

Perhaps. Or perhaps the next breath
or a snowy owl.
Pay
attention.

Standing on our Heads
(in memory of Roger Sale)

"You are old, Father William," the young man said,
"And your hair has become very white;
And yet you incessantly stand on your head –
Do you think, at your age, it is right?"

Lewis Carroll

A flash, a trumpet crash – you, standing on a chair,
bursting open the doors of our stuffy classroom,
pounding at the closed doors of our stuffy minds
with unholy energy, joy swinging through you.
I remember your laughter, your white socks,
that you found toes disgusting, but people generally
worth the trouble. You were so young then
and I was even younger.

Now we are here, Mary
and the other Roger and I, and our hair has become
very white. We are here to say goodbye, to remember
who we were then, to marvel that we have just grown up,
grown old, to be ourselves – it seems you did the same.
Breath comes harder, knees are stiffer, naps
are comforting, still we have forgotten
to stop standing on our heads – it seems you were the same –
we keep writing, painting, loving, turning
the snowball world upside down to see it again
from a new angle. In a dark time we still know
joy, we keep standing on our heads, and it is not right,
but it is necessary.

Crossing the Lake

Fishtime

You knew me
when I was fish
swimming in the round ocean
of my mother,

when her heartbeat
talked drums to me,
when I traced out the rhythms
of blood, playing a treble patter
to her steady bass,
when I flashed fingers,
unfolded the mysteries of skin.

I knew you then,
lawgiver, in each division
of myselves,
in the kind embrace of my mother,
in the round world the size of my
body. You knew me
in my soft bones
until I was ready
to be fish no more,

to die from the round waters
(constricted, tormented, pushed)
into thin air, into the spear of light,
the strange arms of my mother,
exile.

Lawgiver, home me in
the beat of blood,
the round swell of the ocean,
speak to me in water.
Let me breathe
your Name.

When I am three years old

She asks how I have carried her
this little one with her prim hands,
wicked smile,
her dirty shoes, pigtails,
overall slipping off one shoulder –
she is ready to run
to play in the woods
to visit old Charlie in his wigwam
at the end of the block
with her big dog
and they would both get dog biscuits,
and be late for dinner
and lick the bowl the chocolate cake was made in.
She is ready, full of chocolate and glee,
and she asks how I have carried her

through the more-than-70 years since
she was a small person
sitting grinning on the back steps
of the house in Seward Park.

And now in my stiff old body
when I sit like her, hands on my thighs,
feet angled out,
I want to spring up
slowly
go out to find the weeds
spiders mushrooms mud
nuthatches chickadees
any old dogs who come walking along
politely tied to their owners
any old cats who sidle out
to say hello

I carry her laughing
and give her chocolate
and adventures,
I carry her past the gates of darkness
and she
carries me.

Solitaire

I. Awaking

I live in a stew of cries and comforts,
warm arms, warm milk, the riverflow of talk,
lullabies, crackers, bananas, smell of wet wool,
winter lights, all one, all mine,
until the night I wake
into dark in a strange house.

Around me bulk blanketed mounds
I seem to know as mother, father, brother, sister, but
I am the only one awake.
In all the universe everyone sleeps but me.

I am alone, rare, singular.

Solitaire.

I do not cry out. I look and look to know forever
who I am
when no one looks back at me.

II. Island Time

I love the story of the wild horse
in the island's forgotten valley, the story of the girl
who lives alone on an island and makes her own shoes,

makes sorrel soup (years later I will plant sorrel in her honor),

the story of the woman left alone on an island in Alaska
walking wounded through the long dark to bear a child.

Surrounded by family, other kids, jokes, confusion,
the impossibility of being pretty, popular or brave,
I long for an island.

III. The Continent

I live with others, work with others, cook and laugh,
skipping my words into the river of our talk.
Awake at night now in our silent house
I hear my sisters' breathing, creaks and flex
of the old planks, as I go open-eyed
down the hall in the dark to the bathroom.
Awake in the dark I am an old woman and no age,
my reflection hardly showing in the mirror.
Soon it will be gone.

And who looks back at me? The one
who kept on breaking in to every island kingdom,
that other player, inviting me to dance.

Crossing the Lake
(in memory of Belton Dewitt, 1904 - 1994)

When I think of you, I think how love and fear
were joined together in your kind, big body.

Though a child could nestle in your lap, safe from all monsters,

you feared the monsters you could not contain for us,
the storms of growing, bad choices, accidents, the world.

Dear Belton, I remember that summer Margi and I
rowed across Lake Crescent, talking all the way. I

hung on her every word, your daughter, my beautiful cousin,

tall and two years my senior (was I fourteen then?)
How she told me stories!

All my life, I would do anything for a story, and she told me
My Fair Lady, sang me all the songs. I would have rowed
three times around the lake.

We rowed through afternoon and into twilight,
rowed into a dark lake, racing the sun
to shore, giddy with talk, knowing we were in trouble,
as our fathers, those two worried brothers,
paced the shore, looking out for us
into the growing night. Our wise mothers
stayed in the cabin making the dinner we'd want
when we got home. Our fathers imagined us
lost, drowned, raped, kidnapped, wounded, dead.

Oh it was sweet to come home over the waters,
singing, I could have danced all night, on
the street where you live, all I want is a room
somewhere, sweet to be out in the dark beyond the law,

to come home rowing toward the flashlight swung by our fathers,

to the dock and a scolding,
to be safe, to be saved, to be loved
so fearfully.

Dear Uncle, now you have gone, last of the brothers,
taking with you the last of that time,
the hands and feet and love so like my father's. No one
will love me like that again but God,
will hold out such a light to call me home.

True Notes

When I sang
in the Junior Choir of Ascension Episcopal Church
one of the other girls said we'd sound better
if I shut up.

When I sing
Benedictine Priors and Prioresses point out politely
that something has gone wrong in the chant
and those who can't keep on the pitch
should just be quiet.

How can I help it, Beloved,
if I keep wanting to sing to you
in my cracked old tuneless voice?
Can I help it if songs
course through me,
wanting a voice, even mine?

Love finds voice in all her creatures,
the crow not less than the winter wren,
the frog not less than the dolphin.
Those for whom words come hard and stumbling
praise Love as fully as I can
who have them as a gift.

All songs, all words rise up
and are woven into perfect pitch,
into the note and time and joy
that sets the stars to dancing.

Mother at 92

I can write
whatever I want now
to you
love letters
you can't read
or remember
all my words
for nothing
let me kiss you
let me hold you tight.

Nevermind

Forgive me if I stumble
over your name. For the moment,
it's gone. I know you perfectly well,
know who you are and where we've met, but not
your name. Please forgive me if I carry on
talking to you as *you* (Carol? Loretta? Harriet?). Sometime
in the next ten minutes your name
will be reborn in me. Janet! I will say, or
Linda! so good to see you again. We will pretend
the lapse never happened.

I think this is trivial, a side effect
of slower blood flows.
I think this is the beginning
of the walk into darkness.
My mother took it, and my aunt.
Words got lost. Stories were repeated.
Familiar roads changed their shapes.
Nightmares staged themselves
in broad daylight. The mind,
that picker and chooser, sat in the corner
shivering. It was hard to remember
who you had been and who
had loved you. Things were stolen.
Strange people showed up, claiming you,
and you had never met them before.

Sweet nevermind, don't come for me.
I've always been able to count on these
synapses, these elegant connections,
been able to see the whole, the missing piece,
the skewed number, the infelicitous phrase.
I have a library of poems memorized.
I understand the shapes of times and places,
the connections between this and that. I don't
want to walk away from all this competence
into the place where I might forget
God's name. I don't know if I can say
take my memory, my will, my understanding...
nevermind. Be here with me.
Help me to remember your name.

Then, Now

I must have thrown my dinner, thrown
the juice, loved the grand mess I'd made
with my hunger for freedom, running, the green
hills floating out in front of me unclimbed,
but I was two then. You held me safe,
talked stern to me, cleaned up the mess,
made everything all right.
Now I clean up as you at 92 throw juice at me,
your dinner on the floor.
You're right, we've strapped you in,
your worthless children, helpless in our love.
I clean the floor remembering how you were
as you once mopped up after me
hoping in how I might become.

Ashes

To receive
a box wrapped (tastefully) in silver paper:
my mother's ashes.

You weighed hardly more than this
the day you died,
legs and arms like sticks
all the good flesh gone
when you stopped eating
stopped wanting to live
in your deepest bones
(the bones that were broken,
that rejoice).

Nothing of you left anymore
but the grand stories you told
while we polished silver,
we descendants of imagined Norman princes,
about the Sierra ranch where your mother toiled
to keep you in white linen pinafores.
Nothing but your voice naming trees,
hemlock, the Douglas fir, the sweet red cedar
or singing with me, cracked and whispery
the both of us, about the bear who went
over the mountain.

Now the world you lost for years is lost to you.
You didn't want to stay around
for the long dark winter.
You went over the mountain to see
the other side.

I hear you singing somewhere
as I thumb through memories, through photographs,
as I unwrap the black plastic box
holding your ashes,
(nothing to hold).
You have gone into the fire
and I hear you singing.

Scissors. Paper. Rock.

Useless
(for the PazSalud Mission Teams)

She came hoping the American doctors
knew a trick to give back her eyes.
"Someone hit me, hit me bad" and no,
she won't say who, but no sight in the left eye
then six years later, without reason, the right
went bad too. Can you make it good?
We can't. Rivers of sorrow, tears without end
from those unseeing eyes
that have seen too much and will never see
the youngest child, la niña, two years old. That's one
we couldn't help.

She came on Monday saying she hadn't slept four nights
for the pain, the pain visible at her throat, huge
bubble of pain. They wouldn't see her
at the health clinic, we don't know why.
Melissa lanced the abcess, drained it, cleaned it,
packed it, bandaged it, told her to come back Wednesday,
Friday, to be checked and cleaned and packed again.
Friday she brought us all the fruit she could carry,
mangoes and papaya, naranjas, sandias,
an offering of thanks. That's one
we helped.

Mostly we're of little use, you'd think,
looking in from the rich world. A month's worth
of vitamins and Tylenol, some antibiotics,
glasses, toothbrushes, a referral, a kind word.
Little use: we come and go again,
and in a month when the last vitamin is gone
who's the better for us? The doctors think
ah, if we just had ultrasound, x-ray, cat scan,
if we could do a CBC, check liver values, then
we'd be of help.

But no. They are giving us our helplessness,
they who know losses, they who know
the days when daily bread is hard to find,
who know they count for nothing in the rich world,
giving us our uselessness with open hands,
the richest gift. *Not that you healed my wound,
but that you saw me. Not that you could do anything
to heal my eyes, but that you touched me.
You, from the rich world, that you saw me
like a sister, that you took my hand
like a friend.*

Prayer

Sparer,
be saving with me.

Don't
rip through me;

unfold me
gently,
a parcel worth opening,

a gift
worth waiting for.

Saver,
be sparing with me.

Don't
put me
to the test
I will fail.

Turn me
until you find my best
angle.

Look for
my true name,
the name you only know

and speak it.

About Miracles

I could do it still, I could strap on skis,
push out from the pole and dance in and out
around each little mountain, mogul, keeping myself
just forward enough to stay upright,
keeping the balance with my thighs,
each muscle burning, or I could jump on a bicycle
and remember exactly the tricks of balance, pedaling,
the plod of hills, wind in my face going down.
I could, but I can't. I'm well enough to walk
and that so slowly grass may grow between
the one step and the next. Still, I remember,
mind and muscle dancing in my dreams.
Still in the body's wreck I know the body's joys,
and how is this not a miracle?

Prisoners

Every day I wake up naked
to bars, to the guard,
to the gray dust where no
thing grows. I can
not go home until
the trees give milk,
stars weep,
until the birds bring
straw to weave a shirt
and the rats carry in
a scrap of cloth
to cover my loins
and set me free.
Every day I can
not go home.

Every day I wake up in fear
with a hand on my gun, the heat,
the gray dust full of bombs,
the roads lined with faces full
of hate. I can
not go home until
fish dance,
until the fire gives milk,
until a dove flies in
with a scrap of paper
to set me free.
Every day I can
not go home.

Every day I wake up in tears
in my own soft bed,
look out on green
far from the gray dust
and hear bad news. I can
not be at home until
the hills groan,
until a stone gives milk,
until I weave
a scrap of cloth,
a scrap of paper
to set us free.
Every day I can
not be home.

Tide Flats Report

Roads wander down the tongues of salt water,
fresh water mingling with a scrum of bushes, shells,
storage containers, tag ends of rail lines, stench
of rotting seaweed, old wood pulp. Roads leap
over bridges and you're in Tacoma or
twist around to deliver you back to the Interstate
nothing regular here
except

off St. Paul's Avenue,
on J Street a flat, white, plain, huge, fenced-off building
makes no place, no where, no room for wind
or tide stench. Detention Center. Here the living
are kept from living. Here the families come,
mothers wait with children in best frocks, little suits.
They check in, they give their names, they give the name
of the beloved, detainee he's called. Or she. They leave
coats, cellphones, keys, purses, wallets in a locker
and wait in plastic chairs.

I come too, and wait, a visitor for those
who have no family nearby or who have no family
that can visit them. There have been so many now,
Jesús, Juana, Ángel, José, Sandra, Christian, Salvador,
I have blurred the outlines of their stories into one
sad story, how they were picked up, brought here,
how they have been here for months, for years,
in no place, no where, waiting for the court, for their case,
for a chance to say why they should stay,
though unlike St. Paul they cannot claim
to be citizens of Rome.
It seems we do not want them here,
though they have picked our apples and washed our dishes
for years upon years.

We meet in a long room full of screaming children, families,
desperate conversations in Spanish Chinese Ukrainian
How can we pay the bill? When will you know about bail?
We meet with glass between us and speak through phones

that are often broken, I look at the graffiti scratched into the walls,

I look at my watch. I try to think what an old woman can say,
and in broken Spanish, to a young man parched with boredom
in this sterile no place.
How long have you been here?
How's the food? When is your court date?
What do you hope for? Can I be there?

They don't have questions for me. My life is beyond their
imagining, perhaps. The comfort of it, being able to walk out
onto the tide flats or drive out of Tacoma into the world.
After twenty minutes, half an hour, we put our hands

to the glass, he turns back to the guards, to his block, to his bunk.

I walk back, get back my license, keys, phone, coat
and leave. Often it's raining. St. Paul's fills with mud.

But I remember once, when Jesús went to court
we touched, touched hands behind the guards, just once,
no glass between, old woman, young man, beloved,
just once for one moment.
Then they ordered him deported, and I left
to drive back up I-5 in tears and gridlock
to my safe, comfortable home, to dinner.

Sometimes I drive on past St. Paul's and J Street
to the bird sanctuary on other tide flats
with other immigrants, with Common Yellowthroats,
Western Sandpipers, Caspian Terns, Cedar Waxwings,
Wood Ducks, who need no visits, who know nothing of walls.
They fly free.

A Fib

Batter my heart, three-personed God; for, you
As yet but knock, breathe, shine and seek to mend;

John Donne

I would be lying if I said
I didn't miss that steady beat,
the rumble under everything,
thump of the heart's iamb. I am
untuned. The wiring's haywire,

erratic, unticked,
and out of sync.

It would be a fib if I pretended
to like waiting in this unquiet room
I am
sitting with the bully,
the bad kid who slaps all the others,
breaks up the game.

I won't lie to you,
I'm tired of flutter and fib.
Come on: shock, freeze, burn, scar,

batter my heart.

Wolf's Clothing
(For Joanne Craig and Delta)

A child's storybook popup scene:
stout villagers in bright warm clothes carrying sharp pikes
stand around the wolf, who wears a gray, shabby coat
over his rough gray shabby fur.
The wolf is tied down.
The villagers poke at him.
He twists away from them toward the earth
to burrow into it.
The villagers plan to kill him, slowly.

I want to untie the wolf as I want to untie
Jesus, bring him down safe from
waiting for torture to end,
that only ends in death.

When I was four I sat at the top of the stairs
while the wolf my father shot huffed and puffed
up from the basement, the gray, shabby skin
moving again, the long legs of my sister and brother
sticking out underneath. As if
that empty skin had come to life
to hunt down the shooter's child.
Sweet wolf, you never meant me harm.

I don't know what the resurrection of the body means,
except that flesh is hallowed,
the gray shabby fur, the skin is holy,
I won't get to heaven without
my pelt.

Scissors. Paper. Rock.

Scissors

My mother cut patterns pinned to cloth
that we picked out in fights: I like **this** one.
You can't have **that**, the stripes go the wrong ways,
You'll just look fat. We staged the drama
in Fredericks, the Bon Marché, Penneys.
In my fatness and my pique, I stood grumpily
as she pinned the dress, perfectly lifted
from its nest of tissue pattern, tried it on,
adjusted the hem, widened the waist a bit.
I didn't know how to love the gift
she gave me, she didn't know how to love
the awkward girl I was. We both learned.
Now I would walk through fire to find just one,
just one of the beautiful despised dresses she made for me.

Paper

In the obituaries it always says,
"and then she met Larry, the love of her life."
But what if you meet the love of your life
and he's already married, willing to adventure,
write long letters from another country,
arrange trysts in strange hotels? That goes sour
because you get tired of haunting the post office
for letters, tired of being faithless to the wife
for whom he is the love of her life.
All that's left is a shoebox of paper,
a fiction of passion light as air letters
with exotic stamps. And underneath, the rock.
You sit at home alone to read them once more.
All those letters go into the fire.

Rock

Bedrock. Vishnu Schist, Zoroaster Granite,
pattern of fire fused metamorphic rocks
at the bottom of the Grand Canyon.
I carry a younger stone in my pocket now
to ground me. Walking weighted I see
without fear, without shame, the light in these faces,
worn, ordinary, I have been carrying:
my mother's love made real with pinking shears,
the lover who's not my life, the shining souls
in the waiting room hoping their time will turn,
the friends who talk me down the trail, steady me
when I stumble, the ones I help to steady
over the rocks. At the canyon's
dark bottom I walk into the fire, the light.

Journey Song
(with thanks to Antonio Machado)

Traveller,
there is no road.

In front of us the meadow,
the tall grasses of late summer,
asters and Queen Anne's lace,

in front of us the forest,
unpathed, the trees heavy with
unfallen cones, the cedar scented air,

no one to tell us where
to turn or what may lie ahead
beyond the mountains.

But we have come a long way already.
We have walked through the dry lands looking for water,
we have found companions.

Now we share stories, we share food,
we compare maps that show
no road leads on from here. There is no way.

We make the road by going.

A Blessing for Quinn
(One year old, February 20, 2018)

When you're an old lady, as I am now,
when your century turns

may turtles still swim in the depths of the ocean
may the whales still sing

and the dawn redwoods stretch up
from beginnings beyond our imaginations,

and the coyotes claim their lands
in full, defiant song,

and the great blue herons give endless
lessons in patience –

may your children and grandchildren know
how to walk lightly on the earth,

may they know they are part
of all that swims
sings
roots
howls
flies.

May they forgive us.